Contents

Florence Nightingale, a famous nurse

▶ **This is Florence Nightingale. She was born long ago, in the year 1820.**

How are her clothes different from modern clothes?

long ago   year   modern

START-UP HISTORY

◄ • • • • • • • • • • • ►

Florence Nightingale

Stewart Ross

W

Franklin Watts
Published in Great Britain in 2017
by The Watts Publishing Group

Editor: Anna Lee
Consultant: Nora Granger
Designer: Tessa Barwick
Map Illustration: The Map Studio

Produced for Franklin Watts by
White-Thomson Publishing Ltd

www.wtpub.co.uk
+44 (0) 843 208 7460

This book was first published by Evans Brothers Ltd.
It has been revised and fully-updated in line with the KS1
history curriculum.

Dewey Number: 610.7'3'092
SBN: 978 1 4451 3495 6

Printed in China

Franklin Watts
An imprint of
Hachette Children's Group
Part of The Watts Publishing Group
Carmelite House
50 Victoria Embankment
London EC4Y 0DZ

An Hachette UK Company
www.hachette.co.uk

www.franklinwatts.co.uk

Acknowledgements: The publishers would like to thank
the Florence Nightingale Museum, London, for their
assistance with this book.

Picture Acknowledgements: Bridgeman 8, 9r, 10t, 12b,
15; Dreamstime: 17; Florence Nightingale Museum 11,
18, 21bl; Mary Evans: 9l, 12t, 13; P&O Art Collection 7,
20br; Thinkstock: 4, title page and 5 and 14, 19r, 20l, 21tl;
Topfoto: 16, 19l (Fotomas Index), 21r; Wikimedia cover all,
10b.

MIX
Paper from
responsible sources
FSC® C104740

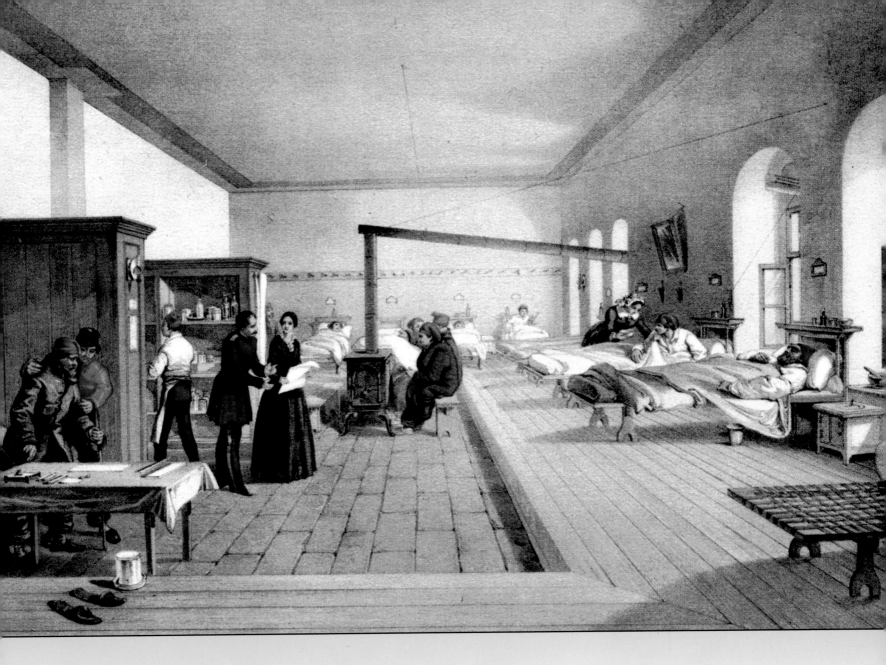

▲ Florence was a **famous nurse**.
She worked in **hospitals** like this one.

famous   **nurse**   **hospitals**

Florence goes to help

In 1854, Great Britain went to war with Russia. The war was far away, in the Crimea.

Florence went to nurse the injured soldiers.

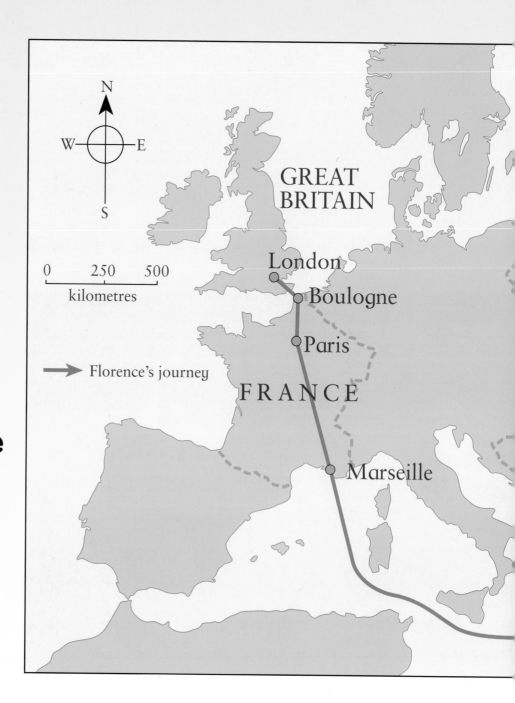

Great Britain war Russia Crimea

RUSSIA

Crimean
Battlefields

Balaklava

BLACK SEA

Scutari

TURKEY

MEDITERRANEAN SEA

◀ **This map shows her journey. She travelled by land and sea.**

▼ **Florence sailed in a ship like this.**

injured   soldiers   map   sailed   **7**
. . . .

Why did Florence go to the war?

▼ **This is a painting of a battle in the Crimean War.
What weapons are the soldiers using?**

painting   battle

▲ This soldier is helping his friend who has been hurt.

Nurses were needed at the war.

▶ This man, Sidney Herbert, asked Florence to go and help. She said "yes" straight away.

weapons   hurt

Florence and the horrible hospital

▶ This is the hospital where Florence worked. It was in a place called Scutari.

Scutari was a long way from the Crimea.

◀ Injured soldiers went to Scutari by boat.

Scutari   boat

▼ **This is the inside of a hospital during the war.**

Scutari hospital looked like this, too.

It was crowded, dirty and smelly.

How many injured soldiers can you see?

crowded   dirty   smelly

11

Florence goes to work

▶ Florence needed medicines from Britain. They were sent by ship.

◀ Queen Victoria helped Florence. She sent kind words and presents for the soldiers.

medicines

▼ **Here is Florence talking to a soldier in Scutari Hospital.**

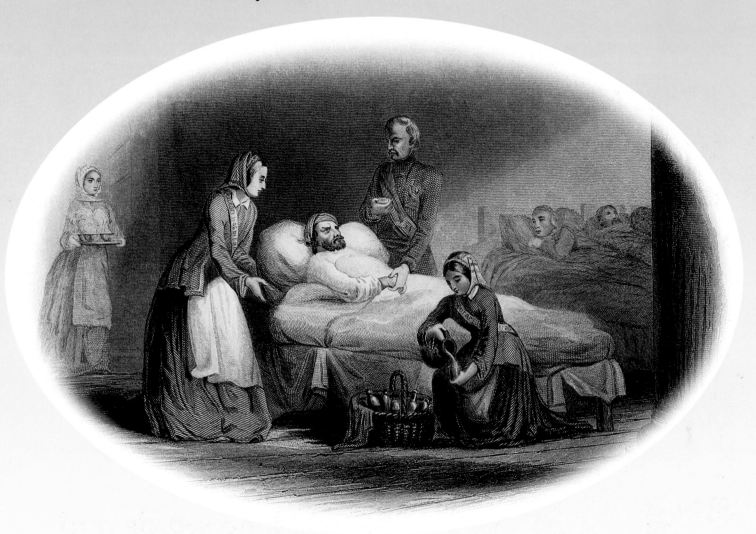

She worked to make it cleaner and healthier.
How is the hospital in this picture different
from the picture of the hospital on page 11?

cleaner   healthier

How did Florence help?

▲ This is the inside of Scutari hospital after Florence had cleaned it up.

There are clean sheets on the beds and a stove to keep the patients warm.

patients

Florence **trained** other nurses at Scutari.

▼ This nurse is working near a battle.

How can you tell that this **photograph**
was taken long ago?

trained   **photograph**

Nursing changes

After she returned from the war, Florence started a school for nurses.

Here is Florence with some of the nurses from her school. The nurses are wearing their uniforms.

16

after   school   uniforms

This is a nurse at work today.
He is wearing a uniform called scrubs.

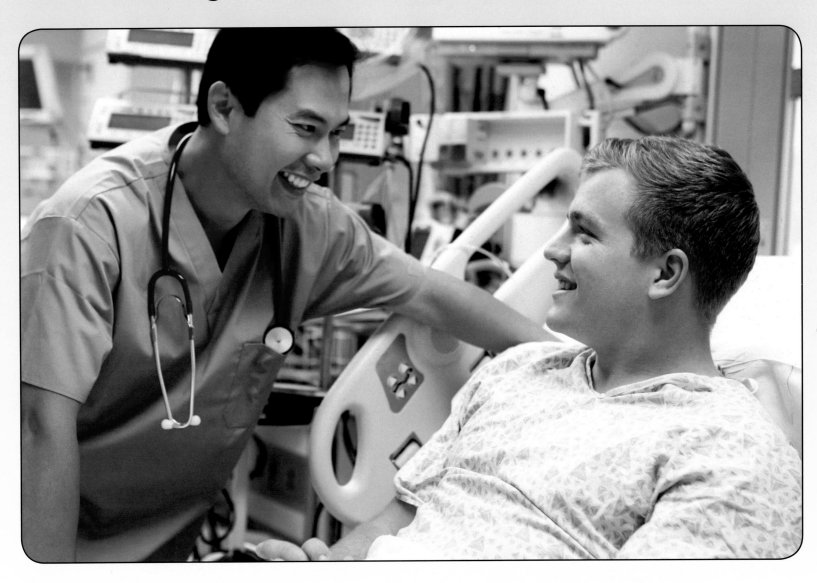

What other differences can you see between this picture and the pictures of the hospitals from the past?

today   scrubs   differences   past   **17**

How do we know about Florence Nightingale?

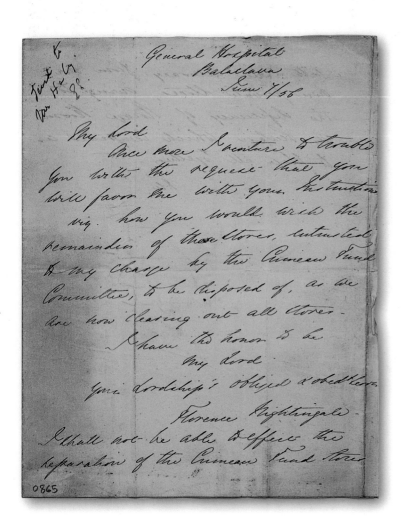

Florence Nightingale died almost 100 years ago.

We can find out about Florence by reading the letters she wrote.

◀ This is a letter Florence wrote to Sidney Herbert from Balaklava.
You can find Balaklava on the map on pages 6 and 7.

died   letters

SAVED BY A FAMOUS NURSE.

A VETERAN'S REMINISCENCE.

[BY TELEGRAPH.—OWN CORRESPONDENT.]

CHRISTCHURCH, Thursday.

WHEN a youth of 17 years of age Edward Bond, now a resident of Christchurch, was engaged as interpreter to the police at Kadakoi, near Balaclava. Under the rigors of the climate he broke down, and after a brief illness was given up as dead by the army doctors in the rude hospital. He was covered over with an army blanket, and over his head the army card announced that he was to be transferred to the "dead tent." On that day Miss Florence Nightingale arrived at Balaclava, and made her first inspection of the hospital. Bond's bed was the first inside the door, and Miss Nightingale paused before it, read the card, and then said softly, "What a pity to die so young." She went to the head of the bed to turn down the blanket, and at once said, "Why, he is not dead." Efforts were made to secure his recovery, and ultimately Bond walked out of the hospital and resumed his duties.

"All that I learnt," said the veteran to a reporter, "from the man in the bed next to mine. If Miss Nightingale had not seen me I would have been taken out to the dead tent. I saw Miss Nightingale just before she was taken ill herself, and I thanked her. She remembered me, saying, 'Oh, you are the boy they ordered to be buried.'"

▼ We can learn about Florence from old paintings and photographs, too.

▲ Newspapers and magazines from long ago tell us about Florence.

newspapers   magazines   **19**

The story of

Use these pictures and words to tell the story of Florence Nightingale.

nurse sailed Crimea soldier war

Florence Nightingale

Where did she go?

What did she do there?

Why do we remember her today?

hospital   cleaner   Scutari   school

Further information for

New history words and words about Florence Nightingale listed in the text:

after	dirty	long ago	past	smelly
battle	famous	magazines	patients	soldiers
boat	Great Britain	map	photograph	today
cleaner	healthier	medicines	Russia	trained
Crimea	hospitals	modern	sailed	uniforms
crowded	hurt	newspapers	school	war
died	injured	nurse	scrubs	weapons
differences	letters	painting	Scutari	year

Background Information

FLORENCE NIGHTINGALE

Florence Nightingale (1820-1910) is remembered for her work as a nurse during the Crimean War. Highly-strung and determined, at an early age Florence set her mind on becoming a nurse. The profession was then almost exclusively the reserve of women of low status. Finally winning parental approval for her career, Florence trained in Germany and worked in London before volunteering to lead a band of 38 nurses to the Crimea in 1854. A formidable organiser (but a poor nurse), Florence set about bringing order to the army hospital at Scutari. However, the appalling death rate there did not subside until a commission had identified and eliminated diseases stemming from the hospital's lamentable sanitation. Florence fell seriously ill in the Crimea and after her return home, now a national hero, she took to her bed for nine years. She devoted the rest of her life to the nursing profession, especially training and army nursing.

THE CRIMEAN WAR

Fought against Russia in alliance with France, the Crimean War (1854-6) soon became a byword for incompetent management and leadership. Anglo-French forces were sent to the Crimea to take the Russian port of Sebastopol and prevent further Russian expansion into the crumbling Ottoman Turkish Empire. A second, Baltic front was opened up to deter Russian expansion into Scandinavia. Ultimately, both campaigns achieved their objectives, although at considerable cost in terms of lives lost and political and military careers ruined. 4,600 British soldiers were killed in battle and 17,500 died of disease. Mounting criticism of the way the war was conducted forced the resignation of Lord Aberdeen's government in 1855.

BALAKLAVA

Balaklava, a small port in the south of the Crimea, was the scene of a major battle of the Crimean War in 1854.

Parents and Teachers

The balaclava helmet, a woollen hood that covers the ears and neck, was worn by soldiers during the Crimean War. It is still used today.

SIDNEY HERBERT

Lord Sidney Herbert (1810-61) served as a reforming minister in the war office from 1845 onwards. He established Aldershot as the major army base in Britain and was responsible for the radical step of sending Florence Nightingale (a personal friend) and her nurses to help at Scutari.

Possible Activities:

Draw pictures of Florence, Scutari and the Crimea.
Make a wall map of Florence's journey to the Crimea.
Make a class frieze timeline.
Find a modern nurse willing to talk to the class about her work. What does she think of Florence Nightingale?
List objects, buildings etc. from the time of Florence Nightingale.

Compare newspaper articles from today and from the nineteenth century. How are they different?

Some Topics for Discussion:

Which tell us more about Florence Nightingale, letters or paintings? What are the advantages and disadvantages of each?
Can we trust 'eyewitnesses'?
What else could Florence have done with her life?
Did she deserve to be a celebrity?
What made her a celebrity?
Discuss other famous people from the past.

Further Information

BOOKS

FOR CHILDREN

Famous People, Great Events: Florence Nightingale by Emma Fischel (Franklin Watts, 2012)
Florence Nightingale: Lady with the Lamp by Trina Robbins and Anne Timmons (Graphic Library, 2007)
The Life of Florence Nightingale by Liz Gogerly (Wayland, 2006)
Popcorn History Corner: Florence Nightingale by Kay Barnham (Wayland, 2010)
Ways Into History: Florence Nightingale by Sally Hewitt (Franklin Watts, 2012)

FOR ADULTS

Florence Nightingale: Avenging Angel (Second Edition) by Hugh Small (Knowledge Leak, 2013)
Florence Nightingale at First Hand by Lynn McDonald (Continuum, 2010)
Florence Nightingale: The Woman and Her Legend by Mark Bostridge (Viking, 2008)

WEBSITES

www.florence-nightingale.co.uk
www.bbc.co.uk/schools/primaryhistory/famouspeople/florence_nightingale
www.bbc.co.uk/programmes/p015j6sc (video about Florence Nightingale's life)

PLACES TO VISIT

Florence Nightingale Museum, London
Bethlem Royal Hospital & Archives, Beckenham, Kent
National Army Museum, London

Index